CW00351890

Canine Quips

from
Mouthy Mongrels

This edition published in 2003 by
Advanced Marketing (UK) Ltd, Bicester, Oxfordshire
Copyright © 2003 Susanna Geoghegan
All rights reserved
Designed by Milestone Design
Printed in China by Imago
ISBN 1903938422

Life is made up of sobs, sniffles and smiles, with sniffles predominating

HENRY O 1862 – 1910

Equality

"All animals are equal but some animals are more equal than others."

GEORGE ORWELL 1903 – 1950

5

Devouring Shakespeare

"Though he had very little Latin beyond "Cave canem"
he had, as a young dog, devoured Shakespeare
(in a tasty leather binding)"

DODIE SMITH 1896 – 1990

stupid men

"Men are clumsy, stupid creatures regarding little things, but in their right place they are wonderful animals."

MILES FRANKLIN 1879 – 1954

9

Call me names!

"I have been called many things, but never an intellectual."

TALLULAH BANKHEAD 1903 – 1968

affectionate people

"*Does it really matter what these affectionate people do –
so long as they don't do it in the street
and frighten the horses.*"

MRS PATRICK CAMPBELL 1865 – 1940

Honesty

"When I want a peerage
I shall buy one like an honest man."

LORD NORTHCLIFFE 1865 – 1922

One glance

"They exchanged the quick, brilliant smile of women who dislike each other on sight."

MARSHALL PUGH

True love?

"By the time you swear you're his,

Shivering and sighing.

And he vows his passion is Infinite, undying -

Lady, make a note of this:

One of you is lying."

DOROTHY PARKER 1893 – 1967

Celebrities

“The nice thing about being a celebrity is that,
if you bore people, they think it's their fault.”

HENRY KISSINGER 1923 –

need me?

"Needing someone is like needing a parachute. If he isn't there the first time you need him, chances are you won't be needing him again."

SCOTT ADAMS 1957 –

25

inspiration

"*I am one of those unhappy persons who inspire bores to the highest flights of their art.*"

EDITH SITWELL 1887 – 1964

25

Knowing men

"*The more I know about men the more I like dogs.*"

GLORIA ALLRED

29

virtue

"My virtue's still far too small,
I don't trot it out and about yet."

COLETTE 1873 – 1954

29

wake up

> ❝ I always like to have the morning
> well-aired before I get up. ❞
>
> BEAU BRUMMEL 1778 – 1840

54

His wit

" His wit invites you by his looks to come,

But when you knock it is never at home. "

WILLIAM COWPER 1731 – 1800

Dogs and cats

"Dogs.... can be made to feel guilty about anything,
including the sins of their owners.
Cats refuse to take the blame for anything -
including their own sins."

ELIZABETH PETERS 1927 –

Sit down

"*I do most of my work sitting down;*
that's where I shine."

ROBERT BENCHLEY 1859 – 1945

Dog food

"The only food he has ever stolen has been down on a coffee table. He claims that he genuinely believed it to be a table meant for dogs."

JEAN LITTLE 1932 –

59

white lies

"*She tells enough white lies to ice a wedding cake.*"

MARGOT ASQUITH 1864 – 1945

A strange family

> "They were a tense and peculiar family, the Oedipuses, weren't they?"

SIR MAX BEERBOHM 1872 – 1956

45

It's a bit early

"I don't grasp things this early in the day.
I mean I hear voices all right,
but I can't pick out the verbs."

JEAN COLLINS KERR 1923 –

The optimist

"The latest definition of an optimist is one who fills up his crossword puzzle in ink."

CLEMENT KING SHORTER 1857 – 1926

Marriage

"It doesn't much signify whom one marries,
for one is sure to find next morning
that it was someone else."

SAMUEL ROGERS 1763 – 1855

49

Wrinkles

"If God had to give woman wrinkles,

he might at least have put them

on the soles of her feet."

NINON DE LENCLOS 1620 – 1705

51

Pity him

"It was a pity he couldna be hatched o'er again, an' hatched different."

GEORGE ELIOT 1819 – 1880

Subtlety

"Never despise what it says in women's magazines:
it may not be subtle but neither are men."

ZSA-ZSA GABOR 1919 –

57

At what cost?

"Experience is a good teacher,
but she sends in terrific bills."

Lesser of two evils

"*Marriage may often be a stormy lake,
but celibacy is almost always a muddy horsepond.*"

THOMAS LOVE PEACOCK 1785 ~ 1866

hard work

"They say hard work never hurt anybody,
but I don't figure why take the chance."

RONALD REAGAN 1911 –

63

A dog's dog

"Arnold was a dog's dog. Whenever he shuffled along walks and through alleyways, he always gave the impression of being onto something big."

MARTHA GRIMES 1930 –

Does anybody want a pup?